The Canadian Rockies

The Canadian Rockies

Introduction by Richard T. Wright.
Photography compiled by Bob Herger.

Published & distributed by
Irving Weisdorf & Co. Ltd.
2801 John St.
Markham, Ontario
L3R 1B4

Introduction

by Richard T. Wright

From the vast dimensionless grasslands of the central plains of North America to the dynamic salt sea of the Pacific Ocean there is an undulating world of ice and snow, rocky peaks and verdant valleys, a land of glaciers and rivers, of wild-life and flowers traversed timidly by sinuous railways and highways.

This is the world of mountains, the massive stone cordillera which forms the twisted, folded backbone of the North Amercian continent. From the isthmus of Panama to the frozen Bering Strait they stretch, a wild rugged line of wilderness, long a barrier to transcontinental travel, and now a retreat from urban living.

Mention the Rocky Mountains and most people will think of this great mass of peaks, 650 kilometres (400 miles) wide and 2500 kilometres (1550 miles) in length. In fact the Rockies are less than 160 kilometres (100 miles) in width, and with the exception of the spectacular section from the 49th parallel of latitude north to the Yukon Territory, the Rockies are reduced to hills once accused of being a railroad press agent's wishful imagery.

West from the Rockies lie the Columbia Mountains, the Ominecas, the Cassiars, the Skeenas, the Coast and the Island Mountains; each of these groups are divided into smaller ranges and masses of peaks. The Purcells, Selkirks, Monashees and Cariboos, for example, are all part of the Columbia Mountains. As impressive as all of these ranges are, they lack the grandeur, the aloofness and the scope of the Rockies.

The Rockies define the eastern boundary with the plains, just as the Great Wall of China marked the border between China and Mongolia, or Hadrian's wall separated the Picts and the Celts. But while the Rockies can be imagined as a wall between two vastly differing geographical zones, the peaks and valleys actually continue for hundreds of miles.

Approached from the west, the Rockies are part of a sea of mountains folding eastward, and the magnificence of discovery is lost. But westbound travellers see them rising on the prairie horizon for hours, a seemingly impenetrable wall of stone jutting skyward from the low foothills and level prairie. In less than a kilometre the flat prairies give way to peaks which soar to 2750 metres (9,000 feet).

These mountains were known to the native Indian peoples: the Cree of the plains, the Blackfoot of the foothills and the Stoneys, who had lived in the mountains for 10,000 years. John Knight, with the Hudson's Bay Company at Fort Churchill, appears to have made the earliest written reference to the people who dwelt in these mythical peaks. In his journal of 1716 he wrote of the "Mountain Indians", who dwelt a great distance away in a land where the mountains rose almost to the skies. For decades these mountains were legendary. The first mention of their present name is in the journal of Leguardeur St. Pierre, 1752, when he referred to the "Montagnes de Roche". In 1754 Anthony Henday, during his explorations of the prairies, became the first European to view the rocky wall.

These and other early travellers did not approach the Rockies as we modern travellers do. It took them weeks to cross the flat plains that stretch a thousand miles from the edge of the Canadian Shield to the foothills. In the northern area around Fort Edmonton they had to cross two hundred miles of muskeg and spruce forest, along a trail that was narrow, dark and boggy, where their only view was the spruce and pine lining the trail and the eastern end of a horse heading west.

Then, rising ahead, were the legendary peaks in their majestic reality — the Montagnes de la Roche. Nothing had prepared them for the experience. The impact of the Rocky Mountain barrier is difficult to recreate or even imagine in today's world, with its television and photographs. A modern traveller with foreknowledge is still stirred by the magnificence of the Rockies. Imagine, then, the awe felt by early travellers who, after weeks and sometimes months of travel, finally faced the ice and snow clad barrier in front of them. Journals of these overlanders record the effect.

Thomas McMicking, leader of the Overlanders of 1862, wrote of his first view as follows:

"On Wednesday, the 13th, precisely at 12 o'clock noon, as the train emerged from a thick spruce swamp and halted for dinner upon a slight eminence, we obtained the first distinct view of the Rocky Mountains. Although we were yet about one hundred miles from them, their dark outline was plainly visible far above the level of the horizon, and their lofty snowclad peaks, standing out in bold relief against the blue sky beyond, and glistening in the sunlight, gave them the appearance of fleecy clouds floating in the distance. The company were enraptured at the sight of them; for whatever dangers or difficulties might possibly be in store for us among them, all were heartily tired of the endless succession of hills and streams and swamps, and swamps and streams and hills and were willing to face almost any danger that would be likely to terminate or vary our toils."

Four days later they had reached the Rockies and he wrote:

"If it be true, as has been said, that 'wherever there is vastness, there dwells sublimity', we were presented with a view at once sublimely grand and overpowering."

The next year, 1863, Dr. Cheadle and Viscount Milton passed along the same route and in his journal Dr. Cheadle described his first sighting.

"Thursday, June 25th . . . On a little bare knoll in the thick wood of the high bank I stopped and awaited the others behind, and had my first view of the Rocky Mountains. A beautiful prospect, and a bluish haze softened off the picture very completely. In the foreground below us rolled the rapid Athabasca between its high banks, clothed in pine, spruce and poplar. Beyond, ranges of hills clothes with pines, and running nearly north and south. Farther still and parallel dimly in the haze stood out the first chain of the mountains 'de facto', backed by still higher ones behind; the sun shone on the peaks. A cleft in the range, cut clean as if with a knife, showed us what we supposed to be the position of Jasper's House and the opening of the gorge through which we were to pass across. It looked not more than 12 or 15 miles off, and we hoped to reach it by sundown."

In December of 1870 William Francis Butler, one of the most descriptive writers of the prairie, saw the mountains for the first time. His description is hard to equal.

". . . and there lay before me a sight to be long remembered. The great chain of the Rocky Mountains rose their snow-clad sierras in endless succession. Climbing one of the eminences, I gained a vantage point on the summit from which some by-gone fire had swept the trees. Then, looking west, I beheld the great range in unclouded glory. The snow had cleared the atmosphere, the sky was coldly bright. An immense plain stretched from my feet to the mountain — a plain so vast that every object of hill and wood and lake lay dwarfed into one continuous level, and at the back of this level, beyond the pines and the lakes and the river-courses, rose the giant range, solid, impassable, silent — a mighty barrier rising midst an immense land, standing sentinel over the plains and prairies of America, over the measureless solitudes of this Great Lone Land. Here, at last, lay the Rocky Mountains."

The formation of the Rocky Mountains began millions of years ago, as an immense inland sea accumulated sediments over a mile deep. For 500 million years the weight of the sediments depressed the ocean floor. Layer upon layer was deposited — layers that eventually solidified into rock. Over 100 million years ago, at a time when dinosaurs roamed the margins of this inland sea, volcanic activity in the area that is now coastal British Columbia began to push some strata east. In the area of the Rockies the strata folded and cracked, much the way a carpet or tablecloth might when pushed. In some places old strata were pushed up over young rock and quickly eroded. Rivers and streams carried the eroded sediments east to the plains in great alluvial fans.

For another 50 million years erosion shaped the landscape, and an inland sea once again submerged the eastern plains. Pressure from the west increased and more folding and compression took place, pushing the mountains further east. About 10 million years ago the region experienced another uplifting and the streams assumed greater gradients, increasing erosion and weathering. The final appearance was created in more recent geological times, about 12,000 years ago, when the Wisconsin ice age crept south, its glaciers scouring out the valleys and passes through which today's rivers and highways run. Erosion and change is a process that continues with each drop of water that leaves the alpine, with every breath of wind and with every lichen that etches its way into bare rock.

The retreating glaciers left many interesting geological forms and features, including the still advancing 200 metre (656 foot) deep Berg Glacier on Mount Robson, and the Columbia Icefield, which can be reached from the Banff-Jasper Highway. Mount Assiniboine, Canada's Matterhorn, is a sculpted semi-pyramidal tower or horn with glacier carved cirques on its flanks, and Lake Louise fills a depression carved by ice. Waterfalls such as Takakkaw, 380 metres (1,246 feet) high, plunge from glacier carved hanging valleys, and kettleholes mark the sites where ice retreated and left tiny round lakes. In Waterton-Glacier, Vimy Peak remains an example of an "overthrust fault", the folding of older sedimentary rock over more recent formations. Roads and trails offer access to all these features, and many more.

Mountains like the Rockies have a profound effect on the weather of any region. Moisture-laden air masses sweep across the coast from the Pacific ocean, carried eastward by prevailing winds. As they are pushed against the high peaks the clouds and air are forced upward, growing colder as they rise, until they condense and fall as rain or snow on the western slopes. The eastward or leeward side of the peaks get little rainfall. This pattern reoccurs at each range of mountains, creating changeable weather conditions and distinct local precipitation patterns. Thus within any range there will be a diversity of climate and, therefore, of vegetation and animal life.

In mountains this diversity is compounded by the various zones of life that occur due to altitude. In the Rockies, these life zones are divided into four. The Arctic, or Alpine, life zone extends from the highest of the ice-covered and windswept peaks down to an altitude of 2225 to 2377 metres (7,300 to 7,800 feet). Here life must often struggle for existence. There are no trees, but in summer alpine meadows cover much of the sparse soil in a rich variety of flowers, and lichens add color to the bare rock. Golden eagles soar in this high country and the pinnacles are scaled only by the sure-footed mountain goat, whose white coat matches the snowy peaks. From the meadows a whistle might announce the presence of a whistler or hoary marmot.

The sound of the whistler echoes to the lower levels of the Hussonian Zone, which extends from the Arctic Zone to the 1,830 metre (6,000 foot) level. The magnificent bighorn sheep is found here, as well as moose, wolverine and grizzly bear. Now the meadows are treed with alpine larch, Englemann spruce and fir, and the flowers no longer huddle close to the rocks for protection, but grow taller, reaching upward to the sun.

This transition continues in the Canadian Zone, which descends to the 1371 metre (4,500 foot) altitude. Here lupines, queenscup and berries are found, along with Douglas maple, white spruce and lodgepole pine. Elk or wapiti frequent the forests, as well as black bear, cougar and migrating sheep.

In the valley bottoms, around the 1220 metre (4,000 foot) level, are the prairie and parkland zones, which have an abundance of smaller animals such as rabbits and hares, meadow voles and ground squirrels, as well as mule deer, valley dwelling moose and a wide variety of birdlife in the willows along lakes and rivers. Grasses are more abundant and the trembling aspen adds a lightness to the forest cover, and in fall a burst of gold.

The Rockies are probably most renowned for the National parks which straddle the peaks. Beginning in the south with the International Peace Park, Waterton Glacier, there are 8 parks, including Kootenay, Yoho, Banff and Jasper. There are also several provincial parks, including Mount Assiniboine and Mount Robson Parks in British Columbia, and the Willmore Wilderness Provincial Park in Alberta. The most famous of these, Banff National Park, has long been the focal point of interest and controversy.

In 1885 the Canadian Pacific Railway was being pushed west as part of the Confederation agreement between British Columbia and the Federal Government of Canada. As the steel rails crept cautiously across slides and avalanche paths and snaked through the river valleys, two railroad men noticed steam rising from the south side of the Bow river. They were found to be hot sulphur springs and the enterprising individuals built a bath house for the tired and dirty railroad gandy-dancers. Business boomed, but when an argument over title ensued it drew the attention of C.P.R. president, Sir William Van Horne. Van Horne saw the value of the bathing monopoly, but as it was not his he took a dislike to it. He encouraged Prime Minister Sir John A. MacDonald to make the area into a park preserve and to develop it at government expense. The C.P.R. would, of course, transport the tourists. As Horne said, "Since we can't export the scenery we'll have to import the tourists." MacDonald quickly agreed, and the two discoverers were blocked in their attempt to get title, though they were compensated. Near the site of the springs the opulent Banff Springs Hotel was built and opened in 1888.

In forming the 6640 square kilometre (2564 square mile) park in 1887, the Dominion of Canada was following the example set by the United States, which had created Yellowstone National Park in 1872. But there was a difference; Yellowstone was created as a wilderness park and Banff was created under what has been termed a "doctrine of usefulness". The park was to be used, developed and turned into a pleasure resort of European flavour. At the same time, resource exploitation was to continue in the form of logging and coal mining. This multiple use policy has narrowed, but the argument still continues today, as groups lobby for wilderness preservation or tourist or other recreational facilities in the park. Banff, and to a lesser extent Jasper, has evolved into a major tourist destination which offers a diverse variety of activities.

The natural attractions of the parks can be seen by a number of transportation methods. The railroad still provides access to some areas as do the Trans Canada Highway and other paved roads. There are 1126 kilometres (700 miles) of trails and close to 3000 campsites for hikers and backpackers. For cross country or nordic skiers there are similar trails for winter use, and for spectacular views there is a 396 metre (1300 foot) gondola lift on Mount Norquay, and another, 701 metres (2300 feet), on Sulphur Mountain. Further north, at Lake Louise, the Whitehorn Gondola offers a panorama of Lake Louise and the Continental Divide. In summer these same lifts can be used as access to high altitude hiking trails where one can wander golden, larch-lined paths and catch glimpses of wild sheep in this magical land. Enveloped in a womb of security, you can float the Bow River on a rubber raft, or you can travel rivers and lakes by canoe. You can see Lake Minnewonka by motor launch, or explore the high back country of hidden valleys and peaks by horse pack.

Several other National and Provincial parks and recreational areas lie west of the main corridor of the Rockies. Yoho National Park lies directly adjacent to Banff and is traversed by the Trans Canada Highway. The 507 square kilometre (196 square mile) park has a topography similar to that of Banff: towering peaks, alpine meadows and deep green lakes, combining to form spectacular vistas. Many of the peaks can be seen from the Trans Canada Highway and 28 of these are over 3048 metres (10,000 feet) in height. Rogers Pass, on the Trans Canada Highway between Golden and Revelstoke, is one of the most famous railway passes in North America. Crossing the backbone of the Selkirk Mountains at 1327 metres (4,354 feet), it averages 940 centimetres (370 inches) of snow a year. Avalanches are common, and even though much of the highway is protected by snow sheds and various avalanche barriers, army howitzers are frequently employed to blast down unstable slopes under controlled conditions.

Glacier National Park is named for the more than 100 glaciers that top the mountains of the Purcell and Selkirk Ranges. These mountains are formed of rock 105 million years old, tens of millions of years older than the Rockies themselves. Hiking trails lead to the glaciers but winter recreationists should be aware that many are in avalanche zones and are potentially hazardous. A few miles further west, in the Selkirk Mountains, is Mount Revelstoke National Park, a 259 square kilometre (100 square mile) preserve which has been eroded and glaciated into a land of rare beauty.

Along the western side of the Rocky Mountains a wide valley stretches half the length of the continent, forming a trench so smooth and symmetrical that it gives the appearance of having been drawn in sand by a celestial finger. This is the Rocky Mountain Trench, a natural reservoir that engineers frequently speak of filling with water in a scheme that would inundate half the valleys of the west for water in the south. The Columbia River flows through part of this trench in British Columbia and forms a boundary between the Rockies and the Purcells. Highway 95 follows the trench and provides access to a region of increasing interest to the mountaineers, the Bugaboo Alpine Recreation area. This area is for experienced mountaineers only; the trail leads to the intricate rockclimbing areas of Snowpatch Spire, Bugaboo Spire and Howser Towers which rise above the glaciers. In winter, when deep seductive powder snow covers the ice fields, the whup-whup-whup of helicopters are heard and then the quiet hissing of skis cutting patterns in the snow. This is one of the continent's foremost helicopter skiing areas, one that has attracted people from around the world to experience the thrill of deep powder skiing.

The parks of the Rockies are many things to the various users. Banff townsite is a good example of the diverse interests. For many travellers it is one of the world's finest resorts, with a multitude of attractions. To me it has meant something different from either of these images.

I first visited Banff when I was about 8 years old in short pants, oxfords and white sweater. I still have those first images in my mind. We came by train, a long, winding string of Pullman cars pulled by great, puffing, snorting, black steam engines. I remember my father being hungry one evening and the porter bringing him a chicken leg and I remember being allowed in the cab of the engine and marvelling at the awesome raw power it exuded. Of the parks there are only large images; mountains higher than I had seen before; Indians somewhere and the grand Banff Springs Hotel. They were overwhelming images for a child.

For many, and I would have to include myself, a visit to the parks of the Rocky Mountains is close to a spiritual experience. These are places to re-create oneself, and feelings much like those of those first travellers surface. Reviewing Canadian art or literature there can be little doubt that mountains have played an important, dynamic role in development of Canadian culture.

Mountain people — those who love the mountains, and live there, or return again and again — are different. They find a comfort in feeling and seeing the mountains loom above, and an ecstasy in scaling the heights. These vast landscapes inspire awe rather than fear with their raw power.

The power of mountains inspires not only artists but men and women who see the mountains as a challenge. They come to the peaks with pitons, ice axes and ropes, to the slopes with skis and to the turbulent rivers with kayaks and rubber rafts. They come to share the mountains with the wildlife and to recapture that feeling of communion with nature on a grand scale which is so often lost to the urban dweller. Visitors here come for renewal, both physical and spiritual, and to test themselves against nature.

The mountains are so many things to so many people that it is difficult to capture them from the viewpoint of one individual. But whoever the visitor, and whatever the nature of the visit, the Rockies are certain to offer recreation and renewal to all.

Cross-country skiing on Lake Louise, Banff National Park.

The Bow Glacier and the leaning St. Nicholas Peak, Banff National Park.

The Scott Glacier descends from the Hooker Icefield in Jasper National Park.

Opposite page: The Banff Springs Hotel sits amid the natural beauty of the Rockies. When it was originally built in the 1880's, it transformed the wilderness into the town of Banff. *Below:* Peyto Lake varies in color according to the seasons. To the left of this scene is Mount Patterson with a height of 3,197 metres (10,490 feet).

Above: Located on the northeast slope of Sulphur Mountain, the Banff Hot Springs were first discovered in 1883 by Canadian Pacific Railway surveyors.

Following pages: The Waterton lakes, named in honour of Charles Waterton, famed 18th century naturalist provide a spectacular view for guests at the Prince of Wales Hotel, seen here in the foreground.

Camping in the Larch Valley, Banff National Park.

Johnston's Canyon, Banff.

Opposite page: Mount Rundle, 2,950 metres (9,675 feet), is a good example of a mountain cut into layered sedimentary rocks. This huge tilted mountain lies immediately southeast of Banff.

Above: The Trans-Canada Highway west of Calgary. The Rockies under cloud cover can be seen in the background. Despite man's progress, this panoramic view from the east has changed very little over the years.

An adult male Mule deer. This species is often sighted around the populated areas of the Rockies.

The Grizzly bear roams the high areas remote from man, and is seldom seen by the visitor to the mountains.

Mount Edith Cavell, 3,363 metres (11,033 feet), is named after a heroic World War I nurse, and dominates the town of Jasper.

Following pages: Banff National Park.

Lower Waterfowl Lake just off the Banff-Jasper highway.

Along the Great Divide, Jasper National Park.

Athabasca Falls in Jasper National Park.

Sentinel Pass climbs between Pinnacle Mountain and Mount Temple, Banff National Park.

Cathedral Mountain, and Lake O'Hara in Yoho National Park.

The golden hue of a cottonwood in the fall.

Opposite page: The golden hue of a cottonwood in the fall.

Below: Alpine Phlox grows in dry open areas of the Rockies.

Above: Lichen, a plant form which gives a thin mantle of color to rocks and trees.

Following pages: Maligne Lake, one of the most scenic areas of the Rockies.

World Cup skiing at Mount Allan, site of the 1988 Winter Olympic Games.

A smile of success lights the face of this climber atop Mount Lefroy; Banff National Park.

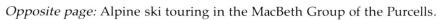

Above: Mount Fay and the Larch Valley. The Larch Valley is a subalpine meadow area just east of Moraine Lake.

Hoar frost on trees at Vermilion Pass near the borders of Banff National Park and Kootenay National Park.

Mount Columbia, 3,747 metres (12,294 feet), the highest peak in the province of Alberta.

The Ramparts and the Tonquin Valley, Jasper National Park.

Bow Lake, Banff National Park.

Spring Beauty, Glacier Lily, Red Heather, and mushrooms, Jasper National Park.

Alpine flowers and mountain falls in the Bugaboos, British Columbia.

Lake Louise, Mirror Lake, and the Bow Valley from the Big Beehive.

The Chateau Lake Louise and the famous poppies.

Preceding pages: Lake Louise and the Victoria Glacier.

Emerald Lake, Yoho National Park.

Mount Assiniboine, 3,618 metres (11,870 feet), the 'Matterhorn of the Rockies'.

Opposite page: The Hoary Marmot is active during daylight hours and retires into his burrow at dusk. These animals hibernate from September until the end of March.

Above: Only one species of tree squirrel is common throughout the Rockies and that is the Red squirrel seen above. Occupying coniferous forests at all elevations they are readily evident from their unmistakable chattering.

Monica Meadows, a remote part of the Purcells.

Spring thaw on Eiffel Lake in the Valley of the Ten Peaks.

Glacier Peak and Mount Ringrose, Yoho National Park.

Mount Sir Donald, Glacier National Park, British Columbia.

Mountain Goat, Jasper National Park, Alberta.

The Consolation Lakes from Mount Temple, Banff National Park.

One of many clear mountain streams near Lake Helen.

Cascade Mountain, 2,998 metres (9,836 feet), and the townsite of Banff.

The Coyote's habitat varies from the grasslands to alpine tundra.

A lone moose drinks at Sandy Lake in the Cariboo Mountains.

Rocky Mountain Big Horn Sheep foraging in winter.

Young Mule deer in Glacier National Park.

Opposite page: Moonlight over Mount Stephen near Field, Yoho National Park.

Below: This view is from the Peyto Lake lookout, and looks up the Mistaya Valley in the direction of Mount Murchison and Mount Wilson.

Above: Alpenglow on Mount Resplendent, Mount Robson Provincial Park.

Following pages: St. Mary's Alpine Park, near Kimberley, British Columbia.

Marble Canyon waterfall in Kootenay National Park.

Mount Lefroy, 3,423 metres (11,230 feet), in the Lake Louise area.

Opposite page: Trail riders inspect their equipment at Berg Lake. The north face of Mount Robson can be seen in the background.

Above: Mount Robson at 3,954 metres (12,972 feet) is the highest peak in the Canadian Rockies. First climbed in 1913 it has been the object of many subsequent expeditions, and is still considered to be one of the most difficult ascents in Canada.

Helicopter-skiing in the Cariboo Mountains.

Ice climbing on Castlegar Falls, Banff National Park.

Takakkaw Falls in Yoho National Park are the third highest in North America. The falls are fed by the Dali Glacier of the Waputik Ice Field and the cool mountain waters then flow into the Yoho River.

The sometimes playful Black bear has often tempted people into thinking it is tame. Although not as awesome as the Grizzly, they are wild and therefore potentially dangerous.

Following pages: Alpine flowers in Kootenay National Park.

Castle Mountain, 2,766 metres (9,076 feet), in Banff National Park.

The Three Sisters, Canmore, Alberta.

An alpine lake in the Purcell Mountains.

Red Rock Canyon and Mount Blakiston, Waterton Lakes National Park.

Summer camping in the Vowell Group north of the Bugaboos.

Below: The Columbia Ice Fields. From this immense ice-cap numerous glaciers melt and give birth to rivers whose waters eventually find their way into the Pacific, Atlantic, and Arctic Oceans.

Above: The Chateau Lake Louise and the lake as seen from the air in winter.

Following pages: A magnificent shot of golden larches in the Glacier Creek area of the Purcells. The larch is the only coniferous tree to shed its needles in the fall.

Mountain Goats beside the Athabaska River, Jasper National Park.

The Cougar, which once occupied the entire continent, is now restricted in range to the wild rugged wilderness areas of the Rocky Mountains, and to the western ranges.

The White-Tailed Ptarmigan. In winter this pigeon-sized bird dons a white plumage which provides excellent camouflage against predators, and aids in heat preservation.

Following pages: Moraine Lake and the Valley of the Ten Peaks.

Opposite page: Sunrise over Mount Cory and the Trans-Canada Highway announces the arrival of a new day in the Canadian Rockies.

Above: A hiking party observe the last rays of light disappearing towards the Pacific Coast. This scene was taken in Mount Robson Provincial Park, British Columbia.

Photographer's Credits

Cover: J. R. A. Burridge; p.10/11: L. Fisher; p.12 top: Scott Rowed; bottom: Garry Fiegehen; p.13 top: Scott Rowed; bottom: Lance Camp; p.14: High Country Color; p.15 top: Gar Lunney; bottom: D. Leighton; p.16/17: L. Fisher; p.18: M. E. Burch; p.19: L. Fisher; p.20: J. A. Kraulis; p.21/22: Ervio Sian; p. 23: Richard Wright; p.24: L. Fisher; p.25: Bob Herger; p.26/27: L. Fisher; p.28 top: Chris Harris; bottom: Gunter Marx; p.29: J. A. Kraulis; p.30,31 top: Bob Herger; p.31 bottom: Doug Leighton; p.32/33: Patrick McGinley; p.34: S. Shortt; p.35: R. W. Laurilla; p.36: J. A. Kraulis; p.37, 38, 39: Scott Rowed; p.40: Harry Rowed; p.41: Bob Herger; p.42/43: Pat Morrow; p.44,45: Scott Rowed; p.46/47: M. E. Burch; p.48/49: R. Garnett; p.50: M. E. Burch; p.51: J. A. Kraulis; p.51: Ervio Sian; p.54: Scott Rowed; p.55: J. A. Kraulis; p.56,57: J. A. Kraulis; p.58: Lance Camp; p.59: L. Fisher; p.60 top: Richard Wright; bottom: Bob Herger; p.61 top: Richard Wright; bottom: Bob Herger; p.62,63: Lance Camp; p.64/65: J. A. Kraulis, p.66: Bob Herger; p.67: J. A. Kraulis; p.68,69: Lance Camp; p.70: Scott Rowed; p.71: Pat Morrow; p.73: Bruno Engler; p.74/75: Bob Herger; p.76: L. Fisher; p.77 top: Bob Herger; bottom: J. A. Kraulis; p.78: Scott Rowed; p.79 top: Bob Herger; bottom: Gary Fiegehen; p.80/81, 82, 83 bottom: Scott Rowed; p.84/85: L. Fisher; p.86: Chris Harris, p.87: Scott Rowed; p.88: Gunter Marx.

Printed and bound in Canada by
D. W. Friesen & Sons Ltd.,
Altona, Manitoba

THIS IS TO CERTIFY THAT

Experienced the Majesty of the
CANADIAN ROCKIES by HELICOPTER!

ON 09 / 09 / 92 PILOT:

CANMORE HELICOPTERS
Box 2069 Canmore, AB T0L 0M0
Tel: 403-678-4802 Fax: 403-678-2176